Fairy Tales
READER'S THEATER
DEVELOP READING FLUENCY AND TEXT COMPREHENSION SKILLS

Written by
Dr. Margaret Allen, Ph.D.

Editor: Alaska Hults
Illustrator: Corbin Hillam
Cover Illustrator: Amy Vangsgard
Designer: Jane Wong-Saunders
Cover Designer: Barbara Peterson
Art Director: Tom Cochrane
Project Director: Carolea Williams

Table of Contents

 = total number of parts

INTRODUCTION

Fluency instruction provides a bridge between being able to "read" a text and being able to understand it. Readers who decode word by word sound plodding and choppy. They are too busy figuring out the words to think about what they are reading. Fluent readers are accurate, quick, and able to read with expression. They make the reading sound interesting. Beyond the experience of the listener, fluent readers are also demonstrating skills that are crucial to their understanding of what they read. Fluent readers recognize words at a glance, group words into meaningful phrases, and move beyond the struggle to decode individual words. They are able to focus on making sense of what they read.

Reader's Theater is an exciting way to help children improve reading fluency without being too time intensive for the teacher. It requires no props and no additional teaching skills on your part, and it is not difficult to manage. Reader's Theater promotes better reading comprehension because children who have learned to read a passage expressively also come to better understand its meaning. In addition, research says that these gains transfer well to new text. Reader's Theater also addresses standards in listening while providing a fun environment for everyone involved. When children practice their lines, they read and reread the same passages. Under your direction, they gradually add more expression, read more smoothly, and find any subtle meanings in the passages.

The scripts in *Fairy Tales Reader's Theater* are designed for fluency instruction. The overall purpose is to provide children with text at their reading level that is fun to read. The scripts serve another useful purpose—they introduce children to stories originally passed along in the oral tradition. Fairy tales are part of our history. However, many children may be unfamiliar with them, and, as they get older, often miss allusions to them in more complex literature. Use these scripts to fill that literary void and to introduce children to stories enjoyed by their ancestors. In addition, all the scripts provide the following hallmarks of a good Reader's Theater text:

- fast-moving dialogue
- action
- humor
- narrative parts

The scripts in *Fairy Tales Reader's Theater* are intended to be read in groups of 5 to 8 children. Each script is prefaced by information that helps you direct learning and is preceded by reproducibles that support extended learning and reading comprehension.

HOW TO USE THIS BOOK

Each Reader's Theater script should be covered over the course of five practice days (although those days do not need to be consecutive). The first day should include some or all of the elements of the suggested reading instruction. It should also include an expressive reading by you of the script as children read along silently. On each of the following days, give children an opportunity to practice their reading. On the final day, have each group read its script for the class.

Four sections that support reading instruction precede each script:

- **Script Summary** provides a plot summary for the script.

- **Reading Rehearsal** features detailed notes for fluency instruction.

- A brief description of each **Part** introduces children to the characters. (See page 5 for more information),

- The **Drama Coach's Corner** provides comprehension activities, suggestions for discussion of the story of the script, and directions for the accompanying reproducibles.

On the first day of instruction, use the background and information about each character to tell children what the script will be about and describe the characters.

Read aloud the script, modeling clear enunciation and a storyteller's voice. Do not be afraid to exaggerate your expression—it will hold the attention of your audience and stick more firmly in their minds when they attempt to mimic you later. Model the pacing you expect from them as they read.

Finish the reading instruction by discussing the fluency tips with children and having them complete any activity described in this section.

Now it is time to give children a copy of the script! Use the following schedule of child practice for a five-day instruction period.

Day 1	After following the steps outlined on page 4, give each child a personal copy of the script. Have children place the script in a file folder and help them staple the pages in place. Invite them to decorate the cover of the file folder.
	Read aloud the script together as a class, in small groups, or in pairs.
Days 2 and 3	Assign children to a group. Have children gather to read aloud the script as many times as time permits. Have them change roles with each reading.
	Move from group to group, providing feedback and additional modeling as needed.
	At the *end* of day 3, assign roles or have children agree on a role to own.

Day 4	Have each group read aloud the script. Move from group to group providing feedback. Have children discuss their favorite lines at the end of each reading and why the manner in which they are read works well. Repeat. Encourage children to check out a script for practice at home. Have children make placards from tagboard to identify their character.
Day 5	Have each group perform its script for the rest of the class (or other audience members provided by buddy classes and/or school personnel).

Throughout the week, or as time permits, provide children with the comprehension activities described in the Drama Coach's Corner. These are optional and do not have to be completed to provide fluency instruction; however, many provide children with additional background information that may help them better understand the characters or setting of the script.

Additional Tips

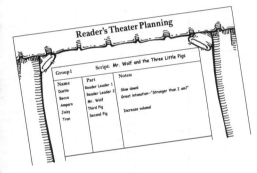

- Use the Reader's Theater Planning reproducible (page 6) to track the assigned roles for each group and to jot down any informal observations you make for assessment. Use these observations to drive future fluency instruction.

- Notice that there are no staging directions in the scripts. These plays are written to be read expressively in a storyteller's voice. If the focus is placed on *acting out* the script, children will shift their focus from the reading to the movement. If children become enchanted with a script and want to act it out, invite them to do so after they have mastered the reading. Then, have the group go through the script and brainstorm their own staging directions. Props should not be included until all fluency goals have been met.

- To fit fluency instruction into an already full day of instruction, it will work best to have all groups work on the same script. This will permit you to complete the first day's activities as a whole class. Children will enjoy hearing how another child reads the same lines, and some mild competition to read expressively will only foster additional effort.

- The roles with the greatest and least number of words to read are noted in the Parts section. The ⬆ and ⬇ indicate a higher or lower *word count.* They are not a reflection of reading level. The Reader Leader parts usually reflect the highest reading level. However, less fluent readers may benefit from having fewer words to master. More advanced readers may benefit from the challenge of the greater word count.

- **First-Grade Teachers:** For the first few months of the year, you may wish to try poems and songs as choral reading in parts to prepare children for independent reading of roles in Reader's Theater.

- **Second-Grade Teachers:** Your children may not need all of the scaffolding presented in the Reading Rehearsal section. Present only what you deem necessary, and move on to the next section.

- Any part can be read in unison. Encourage less fluent readers to pair with more fluent readers for choral reading of a part.

Reader's Theater Planning

Group 1   Script: _____

Name	Part	Notes:

Group 2   Script: _____

Name	Part	Notes:

Group 3   Script: _____

Name	Part	Notes:

ON THE ROAD TO BREMEN

FAIRY TALES

Script Summary

On the Road to Bremen is based on the fairy tale The Bremen Town Musicians. Set the stage by asking children if they have ever had somewhere to go (school, the movies, ball practice) and they stopped to pick up others along the way. Everyone had the same destination but joined the group in sequence. That is what this tale does.

All the animals in the story have the same problem. They all end up with the same solution. But this script has a surprise ending! Before reading the script to the class, write the words *music* and *musicians* on the board. Have children read and discuss the meaning of each word.

Reading Rehearsal

When you read aloud the script for children, have them listen for the following:

- You try to communicate some of the animal in its voice. How would a donkey sound? Point out the word *bray*. Discuss its meaning, and have volunteers model a donkey's *hee-haw* bray. Would it be different than the sound of a rooster, cat, or dog?

- When the animals are happy, their voices sound different than when they are sad. Read aloud the lines **Old Hound:** *Howl! Yowl! Oh, I am old and cannot hunt as I used to. I heard my owner say he was going to get rid of me.* and **Old Hound:** *Oh, thank you! That sounds great!* Have children notice the difference in pace and modulation (there is generally more variation in pitch when you're happy).

Have children practice their "animal voices" to imitate the four main characters of the story. Write one part of the script from each animal on the board. Practice with children reading each part using the animal voice they practiced earlier. Then, copy the script on overhead transparencies, and display them. Read the script, but pause to allow children to read from the transparencies the parts they practiced earlier. Read the whole script again, with children joining in as they are able.

PARTS

Reader Leader 1	Old Hound
Reader Leader 2	Melody Cat
Reader Leader 3	Roscoe Rooster
Dunn Donkey	

DRAMA COACH'S CORNER

Focus on Sequence

OBJECTIVE

Place the events of the story in order.

ACTIVITY

Give each child an **On the Road to Bremen Story Map (page 9).** Have children draw and/or write a key event from the beginning, middle, and end of the story in each section. Then, have children select a partner, and ask them to retell the story in their own words, using the story map as a reference.

The Story of My Trip

OBJECTIVE

Have children relate the trip in *On the Road to Bremen* to a trip in their own lives.

ACTIVITY

Give each child a **My Trip reproducible (page 10).** Invite the class to discuss trips they have taken together or trips they have each taken with their own families. Encourage children to share where they went, the purpose of the trip, who accompanied them, and any interesting events that occurred on the trip. Then, have children complete the reproducible. Display their finished work on a bulletin board titled *Our Travels*.

Name_____   Date _____

On the Road to Bremen Story Map

Directions: Think about the story. Draw or write in each box to show the order in which each character joined the trip to Bremen. Use your story map to retell the story to your partner.

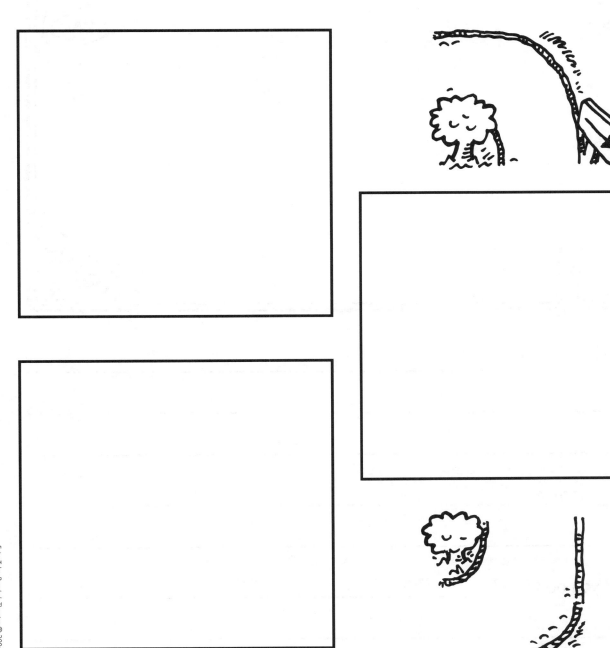

Fairy Tales Reader's Theater © 2004 Creative Teaching Press

My Trip

Directions: Draw a picture of a place you went on a trip. Then answer the questions.

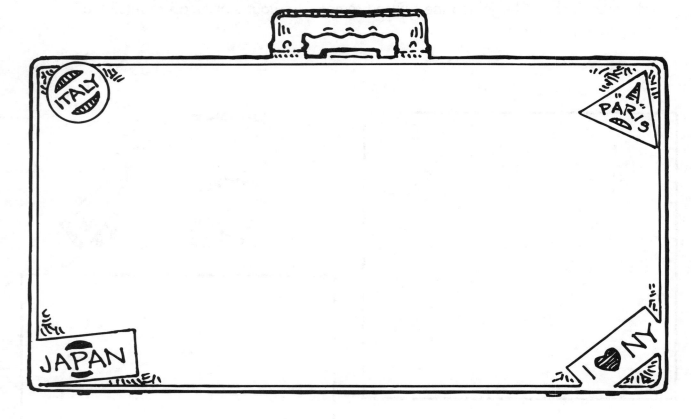

Where did you go? _____

_____

_____

Who went with you? _____

_____

Why did you go there? _____

_____

_____

Fairy Tales Reader's Theater © 2004 Creative Teaching Press

ON THE ROAD TO BREMEN

Retold and adapted by Margaret Allen

PARTS

Reader Leader 1
Reader Leader 2
Reader Leader 3
Dunn Donkey
Old Hound
Melody Cat
Roscoe Rooster

Reader Leader 1: There once was a man who owned a donkey named Dunn. All day the man and Dunn Donkey would go back and forth to the mill.

Reader Leader 2: Dunn carried sacks of grain on his back. It was hard work. Dunn was tired. As he was eating his hay one night, he heard the man talking.

Reader Leader 3: The man told his wife that Dunn Donkey was done! He was too old to carry grain now. The man would have to get rid of him!

Dunn Donkey: I cannot believe this! Every day I have carried sacks of grain for that man. Every day I have worked hard. And now, he wants to get rid of me. I cannot believe this! What am I to do? I know! I will go to Bremen. I can bray. Hee-haw! Hee-haw! I will be a town musician! The road to Bremen is long, but I will take my time.

Reader Leader 2: Before sun up, Dunn Donkey started down the road to Bremen. He had not gone very far.

Reader Leader 3: He came upon Old Hound, who was panting hard.

Dunn Donkey: Old Hound, why do you pant so? Are you okay?

Old Hound: Howl! Yowl! Oh, I am old and cannot hunt as I used to. I heard my owner say he was going to get rid of me. I ran away. But now I do not know what to do.

Dunn Donkey: Why don't you come with me? I can bray. You can howl. We will go to Bremen. We will be musicians together, Bremen town musicians.

Old Hound: Oh, thank you! That sounds great!

Reader Leader 1: So Dunn Donkey and Old Hound started back on the road to Bremen. They walked a while.

Reader Leader 2: Soon, they saw Melody Cat sitting on the road. She was very sad.

Dunn Donkey: Melody Cat, what are you doing on the road?

Old Hound: And why are you so sad?

Melody Cat: Meowwwww! Meowwwww! Oh, I am old and cannot chase mice as I used to. I heard my owner say she was going to get rid of me. I ran away. But now I do not know what to do.

Fairy Tales Reader's Theater © 2004 Creative Teaching Press

Dunn Donkey: Then come with us! I can bray. Old Hound can howl. And you can meow a song. We will go to Bremen and be musicians together.

Melody Cat: Oh, thank you! That sounds great!

Reader Leader 3:   So Dunn Donkey, Old Hound, and Melody Cat started back on the road to Bremen. They walked a short time.

Reader Leader 1:   Soon, they saw Roscoe Rooster sitting on a fence next to the road. He was crowing as loudly as he could.

Roscoe Rooster: Cock-a-doodle-dooooooo!

Dunn Donkey: Roscoe Rooster, why are you so loud?

Melody Cat: You are making enough noise to hurt our ears!

Roscoe Rooster: Oh, I am old. Sometimes I forget to crow! I am practicing. I heard my owner say he was going to get rid of me. So I came here to practice. But now I do not know what to do.

Dunn Donkey: Then come with us! I can bray. Old Hound can howl. Melody Cat can meow a song. And we know you can crow louder than any rooster we have ever heard! Let's all go to Bremen and be musicians together.

Roscoe Rooster: Oh, thank you! That sounds great!

Reader Leader 2: So Dunn Donkey, Old Hound, Melody Cat, and Roscoe Rooster started back on the road to Bremen. They walked until dark. They saw a house with lights on inside.

Dunn Donkey: Let's stay there tonight. I am sure if we sing them a song, they will feed us and let us sleep in the barn.

Reader Leader 3: They walked to the house. The window was very high, so Dunn Donkey stood in front of the window. Old Hound stood on his back. Melody Cat stood on top of the dog. And Roscoe Rooster perched on Melody's head. Roscoe peeked in the window.

Dunn Donkey: What can you see in there, Roscoe?

Roscoe Rooster: Robbers! They have money bags from a bank. They have a huge feast on the table. I am very hungry. If only we could get inside to eat.

Dunn Donkey: When I tell you, make as much noise as you can. Ready, set, GO!

All Animals: Hee-haw! Hee-haw! H-o-w-l! H-o-w-l! Meowwww! Meowwww! Cock-a-doodle-dooo!

Reader Leader 1: Dunn Donkey brayed. Old Hound barked. Melody Cat meowed a song. And Roscoe Rooster crowed as loudly as he could. What noise!

Fairy Tales Reader's Theater © 2004 Creative Teaching Press

Reader Leader 2: The robbers were so scared, they jumped up, ran out of the door, and were never seen again. They left the money and the food on the table—right where it was!

Reader Leader 3: And Dunn Donkey, Old Hound, Melody Cat, and Roscoe Rooster? They never made it to Bremen. They stayed in the house, ate the food, and spent the rest of their lives together—friends forever!

JACK'S MAGIC

FAIRY TALES

SCRIPT SUMMARY

Jack's Magic is based on the traditional tale of Jack and the Beanstalk. Set the stage for reading by showing children a handful of beans. Ask them if they think a handful of beans is worth a whole cow in a trade. No? What if they were magic beans? This story is about magic beans and what happens to the little boy who believes in them. Though a fantasy, it introduces young children to recurring themes in literature of good versus evil and David against Goliath.

READING REHEARSAL

When you read aloud the script for children, have them listen for the following:

- Reader Leader 2 prompts the story forward. Read some of Reader Leader 2's lines for the children, exaggerating the tonal variation. Have children echo read.

- Jack is sad about selling his cow at the start of the story. Point out that you show this by speaking with less expression, in a lower tone of voice, and with a slower pace.

- Note the Giant's repeating line. Point out that it is a variation on the pattern commonly used in the story. Point out that the new arrangement rhymes with the rest of his line.

- Note the Giant's part, and have children echo read it using a projected, deep booming voice. Contrast this to the lighter, higher reading of the Giant's gentle wife. Read her parts together.

PARTS

Reader Leader 1	Mother
Reader Leader 2	Magic Bean Farmer
Reader Leader 3	Giant
Jack	Mrs. Giant

DRAMA COACH'S CORNER

Jack's Friend

> **OBJECTIVE**
> Identify a friend of Jack.

ACTIVITY

Give each child a **Helping Jack reproducible (page 18).** Have children discuss how a friend behaves. Then, have them identify a character or characters who were friends to Jack. Ask children to draw a scene in which Jack is helped by his friend. For example, they may draw the Giant's wife helping Jack escape. Invite children to share their drawing with the class.

Beanstalks

> **OBJECTIVE**
> Explore how a real bean plant grows.

ACTIVITY

Give each child a **My Magic Beanstalk reproducible (page 19),** a **clear plastic cup, potting soil,** a **cup of water,** and **two to four bean seeds.** Have children tell what they know about how real beans grow. Have children look at the reproducible. Explain that they will draw various stages of the plant's growth, and then have them set the reproducible aside. Have children place the potting soil in the cup, tapping it gently on the bottom to settle the dirt. Ask them to place seeds in the soil at the depth indicated on the seed package. Encourage them to place one seed against the side of the cup so they can watch the roots form. The remaining seeds should be planted in the approximate center of the cup. Have children draw the cup and dirt in the first box of the reproducible. Have them water their seeds as needed over the next days. When most of the seeds have sprouted, have children draw the two-leaf sprout in the second box. Wait a few days, and then have them draw the four- to six-leaf sprout in the third box. Wait another two weeks before having them draw the mature plant. (A straw, a piece of string, and a small amount of tape—to hold the string in place on the straw—may help support more mature bean plants, if they start to produce any bean pods while still in the classroom.)

Name_____ Date _____

Helping Jack

Directions: Think about the story. Draw a picture showing Jack's true friend in the story. Talk with a partner about your drawing.

Fairy Tales Reader's Theater © 2004 Creative Teaching Press

My Magic Beanstalk

Directions: Follow your teacher's directions to plant a bean seed. Then draw pictures of your bean plant as it grows.

JACK'S MAGIC

Retold and adapted by Margaret Allen

PARTS

Reader Leader 1
Reader Leader 2
Reader Leader 3
Jack
Mother
Magic Bean Farmer
Giant
Mrs. Giant

Reader Leader 1: See what I have? Magic beans! Let's plant them. They'll grow, and I'll be rich!

Reader Leader 2: Magic beans?

Reader Leader 3: Right! You know, like in "Jack and the Beanstalk." But that story isn't real. There are no magic beans!

Reader Leader 2: Who is Jack? What beanstalk? Would one of you please tell me who Jack is?

Reader Leader 3: Okay. A long time ago there was a little boy named Jack. He and his mother lived in a small house. They were very poor and hungry.

Reader Leader 2: That's terrible!

Reader Leader 1: Right! So, Jack's mother told him to sell the cow.

Mother: Jack, take the cow to town. Sell it. Then bring back the money. I will use it to buy food.

Jack: But, Mother, I like our cow. Do we have to sell her? Oh, okay. I'll do it. I'll sell the cow.

JACK'S MAGIC

Reader Leader 1: On the way to town, Jack met a farmer.

Jack: Hello, sir. I need to sell my cow. Do you want to buy her? She is a very good cow.

Magic Bean Farmer: If she is so good, why do you want to sell her?

Jack: We need the money to buy food.

Magic Bean Farmer: Oh, I have something much better than money!

Jack: What?

Magic Bean Farmer: Look in my hand . . . beans. Magic beans! Take them. Rush home, plant them, and wait for the magic.

Jack: Here is my cow. Now give me the magic beans.

Reader Leader 2: I can't believe Jack fell for that!

Jack: Mother, Mother! Look what I have! Beans!

Mother: Beans? You sold our cow for beans?

Jack: Magic beans, Mother! We just plant them and wait!

Mother: Oh, Jack, my boy. I don't know about that!

Reader Leader 1: But Jack's mother helped him plant the beans.

Reader Leader 2: Did they grow?

Reader Leader 3: Yes! The next morning, the beanstalk was huge!

Jack: Mother! Mother! There is the magic! Look at the beanstalk!

Mother: Oh, my! It goes to the sky!

Jack: I will climb to the top. Maybe there is something valuable there. After all, we cannot live on magic.

Reader Leader 1: Jack climbed to the top of the beanstalk. He could not believe his eyes!

Reader Leader 2: What was up there?

Reader Leader 3: A castle! And near the castle was a hen laying golden eggs, two bags of gold coins, and a talking harp! It said: "Beware of the Giant!"

Jack: What giant? Harp, you are silly. There is no giant. These gold eggs and coins are for me! I will take them to my mother to buy food.

Reader Leader 1: But, just then, Jack heard *thump, thump, THUMP!*

Reader Leader 2: Who made that sound?

Reader Leader 3: It was a giant! A giant who lived in the castle. He was very, very hungry. And when he was hungry he was mean!

Giant: Fee, fi, fum, fo! Who do I smell? I need to know!

Fairy Tales Reader's Theater © 2004 Creative Teaching Press

JACK'S MAGIC

Reader Leader 1: Jack saw the Giant. He hid behind the door. The Giant's wife saw Jack. But she was a very kind woman.

Mrs. Giant: Oh, Giant! You are so silly.

Giant: Fee, fi, fum, fo! Who do I smell? I need to know!

Mrs. Giant: You smell the stew I made for you. Here, eat a big plate of stew with rice. It will fill you up!

Giant: Okay. I will eat the stew. But I know I smell a boy!

Mrs. Giant: Silly man! There is no boy here. Now, eat!

Giant: I am too full to find the boy now. I will take a nap. Snee-*snore*! Snee-*snore*!

Reader Leader 3: Jack tip-toed over to Mrs. Giant.

Jack: Thank you, Mrs. Giant. But I must go now. May I take the gold down the beanstalk? My mother is hungry. She needs the gold now!

Mrs. Giant: Go to her, Jack. Take the hen, the gold, and the harp. We have all we need up here. Take it and go.

Jack: But, will Giant be mad at you?

Fairy Tales Reader's Theater © 2004 Creative Teaching Press

Mrs. Giant: No! He will wake in a better mood; he is really not so bad! Go now. Just to be safe, when you get home, be sure to cut down the beanstalk.

Reader Leader 1: Jack went down with the hen, the gold, and the harp. Then he cut down the beanstalk as fast as he could. His mother came out of the house.

Mother: Oh, Jack. You're back! I am so happy!

Jack: Mother, look. I found our magic—from the magic beans. We will never be hungry again!

Reader Leader 2: Great story! Hey, what about *your* beans?

Reader Leader 3: Wow! They really grew! But, no magic! My beans may not make me rich, but they will make me healthy!

Fairy Tales Reader's Theater © 2004 Creative Teaching Press

MR. WOLF AND THE THREE LITTLE PIGS

FAIRY TALES

SCRIPT SUMMARY

Mr. Wolf and the Three Little Pigs is based on the traditional tale The Three Little Pigs.

Display straws from a broom, sticks gathered from outside, and a brick. Have children examine the three materials. Ask them if they were to build a house, which they would use. This story is about three characters who each build a house, but only one home survives the unexpected visitor!

READING REHEARSAL

When you read aloud the script for children, have them listen for the following:

- Write on the board the wolf's passage asking to come in and the pigs' reply. These two passages are repeated often in the script. Model a crafty wolf voice for the wolf's part, and then an "intimidated" pig voice for the pigs' reply.

- Note how Mama Pig gives her three pigs "rules" for leaving but states them in rhyme. Have children read Mama Pig's rhymes with you, avoiding "sing-song" reading. Next, reread the whole script, with children joining in as they are able.

PARTS

Reader Leader 1
Reader Leader 2
Mama Pig
First Pig

Second Pig
Third Pig
Mr. Wolf

DRAMA COACH'S CORNER

Choices and Consequences

> **OBJECTIVE**
> Consider the choices made by each character.

ACTIVITY

Give each child a **First, Next, Then reproducible (page 27)**. Have children discuss the choices each pig made and why they were or were not good choices for building materials. Ask *Which pig made the smartest choice of building materials? Does that choice make the third pig smarter than the other two? Why or why not?* Have children complete the reproducible and share their work with the class.

That Big Bad Wolf

> **OBJECTIVE**
> Make comparisons between known stories with similar themes.

ACTIVITY

Give each child a **Mr. Wolf reproducible (page 28)**. Have children discuss the stories they know that have a "big bad wolf." (If children cannot name any others, you may want to read to them other stories with a "bad" wolf or have them read the story of Little Red Riding Hood that begins on page 38.) Point out that Mr. Wolf tends to go after people who have made poor choices. Explain that they will write their own Big, Bad Wolf story. Have children brainstorm and tell a partner the poor choice that a character might make and the way it might leave the character vulnerable to the wolf. Encourage them to brainstorm words they could use in their story, such as *scared, eaten,* or *brave*. Write these words on **chart paper** for children to use in their stories. Have children use their ideas to complete the story on the reproducible. Invite children to share their stories with the class.

First, Next, Then

Directions: Look at the houses. Each time Mr. Wolf paid a visit, he blew on a pig's house. Draw or write about what happened.

The wolf huffed and puffed on the straw house.

The wolf huffed and puffed on the stick house.

The wolf huffed and puffed on the brick house.

Name_____ Date _____

Mr. Wolf and the Three Little _____

Directions: Add a new chapter to Mr. Wolf's story. Which animal did he try to eat next? Was it big or little? What kind of home did it build? How did it get away from the wolf? Or, did it get away? Use the story of the Three Little Pigs to help you write your story.

Once upon a time,

there were three _____.

There was not much food, so the three_____left home.

They _____

_____

_____

_____

_____

_____

_____

_____

_____

MR. WOLF AND THE THREE LITTLE PIGS

Retold and adapted by Margaret Allen

PARTS

Reader Leader 1
Reader Leader 2
Mama Pig
First Pig
Second Pig
Third Pig
Mr. Wolf

First Pig:	Oh, Mother, dear. Please come here.
Second Pig:	There isn't much food left. I think it is time for us to go off and find our way in the world.
Third Pig:	We are all packed. We'll leave right away.
Mama Pig:	I'll always love you. I'll always be near. I have some advice to give you before you leave.
All Three Pigs:	We love you, too. We hate to go away.
Mama Pig:	My three little pigs, my piggies so sweet, always stay clean. And wash your feet!
All Three Pigs:	We can do that, Mama. We can stay clean!
Mama Pig:	And brush your teeth. Curl your tail. Write every day. I'll check the mail.
All Three Pigs:	We can do that, Mama. We can stay clean! We'll brush and curl and write every day.
Reader Leader 1:	And with that, the three pigs gathered their bags and were off.

Mr. Wolf and the Three Little Pigs

Reader Leader 2: The first little pig met a man with straw.

First Pig: Just what I need! Straw is perfect for the fashionable country home! I will buy the straw to build my house today.

Reader Leader 1: The second little pig met a man with sticks.

Second Pig: Just what I need! A house made of sticks will have that airy, open feel to it! I will buy the sticks to build my house today.

Reader Leader 2: The third little pig met a man with bricks.

Third Pig: Just what I need! A house made of bricks will last in the worst of storms, the greatest of winds, and it holds the heat in nicely in the winter! I'll buy the bricks to build my house today.

Reader Leader 1: And so all three pigs had new homes. All was well. Each pig went to work each morning and came home to his house every evening.

Reader Leader 2: Each pig stayed clean. Each pig brushed his teeth. Each pig curled his tail. And each pig wrote to Mama every day.

Reader Leader 1: But then, one day, things started to change!

Fairy Tales Reader's Theater © 2004 Creative Teaching Press

MR. WOLF AND THE THREE LITTLE PIGS

Reader Leader 2: The first little pig was in his straw house. He was cooking supper. There was a knock at the door.

First Pig: Who is it?

Mr. Wolf: Little pig, little pig. Let me come in, or I'll huff and puff, and blow your house in!

First Pig: Oh, no! Mr. Wolf, you may not come in. Not by the hair of my chinny-chin-chin!

Reader Leader 1: The wolf huffed and puffed. The straw scattered in all directions. The first little pig jumped up and ran. He ran and he ran to his Mama's again.

Mama Pig: You are safe now. Let's eat. I'll cut my bread in two.

Reader Leader 2: The second little pig was in his stick house. He was watching TV. There was a knock at the door.

Second Pig: Who is it?

Mr. Wolf: Little pig, little pig. Let me come in, or I'll huff and puff, and blow your house in!

Second Pig: Oh, no! Mr. Wolf, you may not come in. Not by the hair of my chinny-chin-chin!

Reader Leader 1: The wolf huffed and puffed. Sticks flew off in all directions. The second little pig jumped up and ran. He ran and he ran to his Mama's again.

Fairy Tales Reader's Theater © 2004 Creative Teaching Press

Mama Pig: Oh, my little piggy. You're as safe as can be. Stay here with us. I'll cut the bread into three.

Reader Leader 2: The third little pig was in his brick house. He was reading a book about wolves. There was a knock at the door.

Third Pig: Who is it?

Mr. Wolf: Little pig, little pig. Let me come in, or I'll huff and puff, and blow your house in!

Third Pig: Oh, no! Mr. Wolf, you may not come in. Not by the hair of my chinny-chin-chin!

Reader Leader 1: The wolf huffed and puffed.

Mr. Wolf: Something is wrong!

Reader Leader 2: He blew and he blew.

Mr. Wolf: Why won't it fall?

Reader Leader 1: No matter how hard he puffed, the brick house would not break in two.

Third Pig: What's wrong, Mr. Wolf? Can't blow my house in? Now please go away. I'm going back to my den.

Reader Leader 2: But the wolf would not give up. He climbed on the roof. He started down the chimney.

Fairy Tales Reader's Theater © 2004 Creative Teaching Press

MR. WOLF AND THE THREE LITTLE PIGS

Mr. Wolf: Hmmm! What's that smell? It is kind of smokey.

Reader Leader 1: Mr. Wolf went further down the chimney.

Mr. Wolf: What is that smell? It smells like roast . . . turkey? Boy, am I hot! Yikes! That smell is me!

Third Pig: Mr. Wolf, did I happen to say I lit a fire in my den today? Good-bye Mr. Wolf . . . and stay away!

Reader Leader 2: Mr. Wolf ran away as fast as he could. He never bothered the pigs again.

Third Pig: I think in my next letter, I'll tell Mama and my brothers to come live with me. That wolf is through!

Reader Leader 1: So all of the pigs were together at last.

Reader Leader 2: With food, curly tails, and no thought of the past!

Fairy Tales Reader's Theater © 2004 Creative Teaching Press

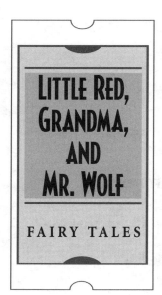

LITTLE RED, GRANDMA, AND MR. WOLF

FAIRY TALES

SCRIPT SUMMARY

Little Red, Grandma, and Mr. Wolf is based on the traditional fairy tale Little Red Riding Hood. Gather different versions of the fairy tale from your school library, and display them in your classroom. Ask children if they are familiar with the story, and ask them to tell what they know. Remind children that since fairy tales were often passed down orally, the stories may not always be exactly the same. Play a quick game of "Gossip" to demonstrate this idea. Divide the class into two groups. Start a secret with the leader of each group, and have each child pass it around the circle. Does the secret heard by the last person in each group match the group's initial secret? This script is for Reader's Theater, so it may not exactly match other familiar versions.

READING REHEARSAL

When you read aloud the script for children, have them listen for the following:

- The wolf's voice should sound earnest when he is fooling Grandma and Little Red. Model speaking very clearly and in a higher-than-normal voice. Explain that highly pitched voices can communicate "trust me" while low pitched voices may communicate "obey me." (The opposite may be true for volume.) Pick one of the wolf's lines, and model the reading both ways. Ask children to pick which they would be more likely to trust.

- Point out the dialogue between Mr. Wolf (speaking in a high falsetto voice) and Little Red. Explain that in this section, Mr. Wolf's voice goes even higher since he is pretending to be an old woman.

- Mr. Hunter's parts are read with great excitement and worry. Note that your pace picks up and your tone varies more. Model the line **Mr. Hunter:** *Grandma, Brutus came to get me. What is the problem in there?*

- Introduce the word *cottage*, and explain that a cottage is a very small, simply made, one- or two-room house. Cottages are common today as vacation homes, but they would have been a comfortable home for a small family many years ago when houses were much more difficult to build.

- Point out that Brutus is Grandma's dog.

PARTS

Reader Leader 1	Grandma
Reader Leader 2	Little Red
Reader Leader 3	Little Red's Mother
Mr. Hunter	Mr. Wolf

DRAMA COACH'S CORNER

Walking Alone

OBJECTIVE

Discuss safety rules for walking alone.

ACTIVITY

Give each child a **Stranger Danger reproducible (page 36).** Have children discuss the two important rules from the story for children walking alone. Point out that whenever possible, they would want to walk with an adult and that their parents may have additional rules for their walk, but that these two rules are a good place to start. Have children look at the pictures and write the rule that Little Red forgot under each picture.

What Happened Next?

OBJECTIVE

Extend the story of Little Red Riding Hood.

ACTIVITY

Give each child a **What Happened Next? reproducible (page 37).** Ask children to consider what happened to the big bad wolf. Ask *Did he escape? Did he go to jail? Did he have to pay back what he robbed? Did he have to say sorry to Grandma and Little Red? How does he feel now that he's been caught?* Have children write their responses under each box on the reproducible.

Stranger Danger

Directions: Little Red forgot two important rules when walking alone. Look at the two pictures. Write the "Stranger Danger" rule Little Red forgot under each picture.

_____

_____

_____

_____

_____

_____

Fairy Tales Reader's Theater © 2004 Creative Teaching Press

Name _____   Date _____

What Happened Next?

Directions: Mr. Hunter caught the big bad wolf. What happened to the wolf next? Draw what happened in the next two boxes. Write about it underneath the boxes.

Mr. Hunter and Brutus
caught Mr. Wolf.

_____
_____
_____

_____
_____
_____

LITTLE RED, GRANDMA, AND MR. WOLF

Retold and adapted by Margaret Allen

PARTS

Reader Leader 1
Reader Leader 2
Reader Leader 3
Mr. Hunter
Grandma
Little Red
Little Red's Mother
Mr. Wolf

Reader Leader 1: Deep in the woods was a tiny cottage. In that cottage lived a pretty little girl and her mother.

Reader Leader 2: Because the little girl was so sweet, everyone loved her. Because she had such long red hair, everyone called her Little Red.

Reader Leader 3: Little Red's grandma loved her best of all. She made her a little red velvet cape with a hood. Little Red wore it every day. Soon people called her Little Red Riding Hood—even her mother.

Little Red's Mother: Good morning, my Little Red Riding Hood. Get up and get dressed. Grandma is ill and needs our help.

Little Red: What? Grandma is ill? What can I do to help her?

Little Red's Mother: Go to her cottage on the other side of the woods. Take this basket of fresh muffins, butter, and juice to her. Oh, and Little Red, wear your red riding hood. It is still cool outside.

Little Red: Of course, Mother. I always wear it. I love it!

Fairy Tales Reader's Theater © 2004 Creative Teaching Press

Little Red's Mother: And, Little Red, do not stop to talk to strangers. And do not get off the main path.

Little Red: Yes, Mother.

Reader Leader 1:   Little Red Riding Hood started down the path. It was a beautiful day. But, someone else had started down the same path as Little Red Riding Hood— Mr. Wolf!

Reader Leader 2:   Big, *bad* Mr. Wolf!

Mr. Wolf: Good morning, little girl. What a pretty red riding hood, and what pretty red hair. How are you today?

Reader Leader 3:   Little Red forgot what her mother had said. She stopped and spoke to the stranger.

Little Red: And good morning to you, too, Mr. . . . uh . . .

Mr. Wolf: Wolf! You can call me Mr. Wolf. Where are you going this cool morning?

Little Red: I am going to Grandma's house. She lives on the other side of the woods. She is ill.

Mr. Wolf: What a shame!

Little Red: Yes, I know. So I am bringing her this basket of fresh muffins, butter, and juice.

Mr. Wolf: How nice of you! But, wouldn't she love some fresh flowers, too? I see lots of pretty flowers over there, on the other path.

Little Red: Why, yes! She would love flowers. I'll go pick some.

Reader Leader 1:   Little Red Riding Hood forgot something else. She forgot that her mother said to stay on the main path.

Reader Leader 2:   And that means trouble! While Little Red picked flowers, Mr. Wolf ran to Grandma's cottage. He knocked on her door.

Grandma: Who is there?

Reader Leader 3:   Mr. Wolf answered in a high squeaky voice.

Mr. Wolf: Grandma, it's me, Little Red. I have a basket of muffins, butter, and juice for you.

Grandma: Oh, dear Little Red. Do come in. You will be my best medicine!

Reader Leader 1:   Just then, Mr. Wolf burst in. He tied Grandma up. Then he started to rob her cottage. But right in the middle of stealing her silver, there was another knock at the door.

Fairy Tales Reader's Theater © 2004 Creative Teaching Press

LITTLE RED, GRANDMA, AND MR. WOLF

Reader Leader 2: Mr. Wolf peeked out of the window. He saw Little Red Riding Hood. He ran to Grandma's dresser. He put on a gown and bonnet. Then he jumped in bed.

Little Red: Hello . . . Hello, Grandma. It's me, Little Red. I am here to help you. May I come in?

Reader Leader 3: Mr. Wolf spoke in a high squeaky voice.

Mr. Wolf: Oh, yes, dear. Do come in!

Little Red: My, Grandma, what big ears you have!

Mr. Wolf: The better to hear you with, my dear.

Little Red: My, Grandma, what big eyes you have!

Mr. Wolf: The better to see you with, my dear.

Little Red: My, Grandma, what big hands you have!

Mr. Wolf: The better to *grab* you with, my dear!

Reader Leader 1: And with that, Mr. Wolf jumped out of bed. He grabbed Little Red. He tied her up with Grandma. Then he went back to stealing the silver.

Little Red: Oh, Grandma, I am so sorry! I did not do what Mother said. I talked to a stranger. I left the path in the woods. I only wanted to pick flowers for you. I did not mean to hurt you!

Grandma: Don't worry, my dear. While Mr. Wolf was busy trying to fool you, I fooled him! I sent Brutus to Mr. Hunter's house. He will be here soon to help us.

Reader Leader 2: Mr. Hunter was Grandma's neighbor. He knew Grandma's dog, Brutus, and he was always ready to help his friends in the woods.

Reader Leader 3: Mr. Hunter ran with the dog back to the cottage. He called out to Grandma.

Mr. Hunter: Grandma, Brutus came to get me. What is the problem in there?

Grandma: The wolf! The wolf! The big bad wolf!

Reader Leader 1: Mr. Hunter broke down the door and went in with Brutus.

Mr. Hunter: Get him, Brutus! Get that robber. Then I will take him to jail.

Reader Leader 2: Brutus jumped on Mr. Wolf. Mr. Hunter caught him.

Mr. Hunter: So we have you, Mr. Wolf! Grandma, Little Red, this is a very bad wolf! He has robbed three other cottages this week. Now we have you, you big bad wolf!

Reader Leader 3: So Grandma and Little Red were safe. And ever since then, Little Red *always* listens to her mother!

RUN, RUN, RUN!

FAIRY TALES

SCRIPT SUMMARY

Run, Run, Run! is based on the traditional tale The Gingerbread Man. To set the stage for reading, ask children if they were ever lonely and wished for or created a make-believe friend in their mind. In this story, the man and woman do more than create a make-believe boy, they make one out of gingerbread!

READING REHEARSAL

When you read aloud the script for children, have them listen for the following:

- Discuss how each of the characters sounds when he or she is trying to stop Ginger B. Point out that these characters will probably increase their volume and pace as they show with their voice their desire to get Ginger B to pay attention to them.

- Ginger B has a four-line rhyme. Write it on the board, and read it with expression.

- Point out that the two-line part each character chasing Ginger B says should show that he or she is so tired! The characters' voices are lower in tone and slower in pace.

PARTS

Reader Leader 1   Mr. Lonely
Reader Leader 2   Ima Lonely
Reader Leader 3   Bert Bear
Ginger B   Felix Fox

DRAMA COACH'S CORNER

Meet My Friend

OBJECTIVE
Consider how new friends are made and practice social skills.

ACTIVITY

Give each child a **Making Friends reproducible (page 45).** Ask children to think about how Ima Lonely and Mr. Lonely felt before they had Ginger B. How would the children feel if they had no friends to play with? Have children discuss how they could reach out to a new child and make him or her feel welcome. Then, have them complete the reproducible as if they were introducing a new friend to their classmates.

Retell It!

OBJECTIVE
Demonstrate story comprehension through a retelling of the story on a graphic organizer.

ACTIVITY

Give each child a **Retell It! reproducible (page 46).** Have children discuss the story and then illustrate it on the reproducible. Point out that the first box is the one at the top. Display children's finished work on a bulletin board titled *Run, Run, Run!*

Name______________________________ Date ______________

Making Friends

HELLO
My name is

Directions: Think about how you could welcome a new friend to your school. Draw him or her in the box. Write about how you could introduce your new friend to others.

Meet my new friend, ______________________________.

My new friend ______________________ is ____________ years old.

____________________ can ______________________________

____

I like my new friend because ______________________________

____

____

____

Name_____ Date _____

Retell It!

Directions: Retell the story of *Run, Run, Run!* by drawing pictures or writing in the boxes provided.

Fairy Tales Reader's Theater © 2004 Creative Teaching Press

Run, Run, Run!

Retold and adapted by Margaret Allen

PARTS

Reader Leader 1
Reader Leader 2
Reader Leader 3
Ginger B
Mr. Lonely
Ima Lonely
Bert Bear
Felix Fox

Reader Leader 1: Mr. Lonely lived with his wife Ima in a house near the river. It was a very quiet place to live.

Ima Lonely: It is so quiet here. Do you know what we need to liven up the place?

Mr. Lonely: No, what?

Ima Lonely: A child!

Mr. Lonely: A child? There are no children around here. Where will you get a child?

Ima Lonely: I'll make us one! I will make us a nice gingerbread child. A boy, I think! We will call him Ginger B.

Reader Leader 2: And Ima spent all day in the kitchen. She made a big batch of gingerbread. She shaped it into a boy. She put candy dots for a mouth, raisins for eyes, and a cherry for a nose. She popped it into the oven.

RUN, RUN, RUN!

Ima Lonely: Mr. Lonely, I am going to take a nap. The gingerbread is baking. Whatever you do, don't open the oven.

Reader Leader 3: While Ima Lonely napped, the gingerbread baked. The house smelled SO good!

Mr. Lonely: My, that smells good. I wonder if it is done. Maybe I'll take a look.

Reader Leader 1: Mr. Lonely opened the oven. Ginger B was done all right! He popped out of the oven.

Ginger B: Wow! Look at me. I'm a gingerbread boy!

Mr. Lonely: Yes, we are so happy to have you in our home!

Reader Leader 2: Ginger B did not listen. He ran out of the kitchen and out of the house.

Mr. Lonely: Stop, Ginger B, stop! You are our boy! Stop now!

Ginger B: Run, run, run. Can't catch me! Run, run, run, I'm Ginger B!

Mr. Lonely: Stop! Stop! OH, I am too tired. I will have to sit down and rest.

Fairy Tales Reader's Theater © 2004 Creative Teaching Press

RUN, RUN, RUN!

Reader Leader 3: Ima got up from her nap. She saw the open oven door. She saw the open front door. She knew something was wrong. She ran to catch up with Mr. Lonely and Ginger B.

Ima Lonely: Where is Ginger B?

Mr. Lonely: Gone! He thinks he's a man. He ran away.

Ima Lonely: A man? He is our boy! I'll catch him. Ginger B, Ginger B. Come to me!

Ginger B: Run, run, run. Can't catch me! Run, run, run, I'm Ginger B! I ran away from Mr. Lonely. And I can run away from you, too. I can. I can.

Ima Lonely: Stop! Stop! OH, I am too tired. I will have to sit down and rest.

Reader Leader 1: Ginger B ran on until he met Bert Bear.

Bert Bear: Ginger B, Mr. and Mrs. Lonely are looking for you. You are their boy. Stop now. I will take you to them.

Ginger B: Run, run, run. Can't catch me! Run, run, run, I'm Ginger B! I ran away from Mr. Lonely and Ima. And I can run away from you, too. I can. I can.

Fairy Tales Reader's Theater © 2004 Creative Teaching Press

Bert Bear: Stop! Stop! OH, I am too tired. I will have to sit down and rest.

Reader Leader 2: Ginger B ran on until he met Felix Fox.

Felix Fox: Say, aren't you Mr. and Mrs. Lonely's boy? I heard they have a new gingerbread son. Want me to take you to them?

Ginger B: I'm going, I'm gone! If you want to take me to them, run and catch me.

Reader Leader 3: And Ginger B started to run again. But he called to Felix Fox.

Ginger B: Run, run, run. Can't catch me! Run, run, run, I'm Ginger B! I ran away from Mr. Lonely and Ima. I ran away from Bert Bear. And I can run away from you, too. I can. I can.

Felix Fox: Stop! Stop! OH, I am too tired. I will have to sit down and rest.

Reader Leader 1: But Ginger B did not stop to rest. He ran so fast, he did not watch where he was going. He ran off the bank. He fell into the river.

Fairy Tales Reader's Theater © 2004 Creative Teaching Press

Ginger B: Help, Mr. Lonely! Help, Ima! Bert, help me! Felix, help me! I'm drowning!

Reader Leader 2:   They all came running. They linked hand in hand, across the river—Mr. Lonely, Ima Lonely, Bert Bear, and Felix Fox. They saved Ginger B.

Bert and Felix: Boy, that was a close call!

Mr. Lonely and Ima: Our boy, our boy. You are safe!

Ginger B: Yes, I am your boy. You made me. And even though I ran away, you saved me. I will always be your boy!

Reader Leader 3:   They went home. Mr. and Mrs. Lonely invited Bert and Felix to the house to eat. Ima baked some gingerbread—not a gingerbread man, not a gingerbread boy, just gingerbread. And they all enjoyed it together!

Fairy Tales Reader's Theater © 2004 Creative Teaching Press

ALL BY MYSELF!

FAIRY TALES

SCRIPT SUMMARY

All by Myself! is based on the traditional tale The Little Red Hen. To set the stage for reading, ask children if they ever had a job to do and wanted help. Did their friends help them? Should friends help each other? Why or why not? This is the story about a character who needed help . . . and didn't get it!

READING REHEARSAL

When you read aloud the script for children, have them listen for the following:

- Dandy Duck, Kit Cat, and Percy Pig have repeated responses for not offering help. Model exaggerated exhaustion and a high, nasal whine.

- Read the two-line rhyme that Little Red Hen uses each time she moves to the next stage of wheat preparation. She speaks expressively and shows patience by speaking in a slightly slower than normal pace.

Have children practice their "animal voices" to imitate the four main characters of the story. Write one part of the script from each animal on the board. Practice with children reading each part using the animal voice they practiced earlier. Then, copy the script on overhead transparencies, and display them. Read the script, but pause to allow children to read from the transparencies the parts they practiced earlier. Read the whole script again, with children joining in as they are able.

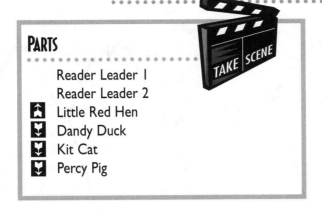

PARTS

Reader Leader 1
Reader Leader 2
Little Red Hen
Dandy Duck
Kit Cat
Percy Pig

Drama Coach's Corner

Story Sequence

OBJECTIVE
Recall the sequence of the story.

ACTIVITY

Give each child a **Little Red Hen reproducible (page 54)**. Have children recall the steps Little Red Hen used to go from wheat seeds to a loaf of bread. Then, have them write about each step on one of Little Red Hen's feathers. Invite children to share their completed work with the class. You may wish to invite early finishers to color in the hen.

To the Rescue!

OBJECTIVE
Have children relate story themes to their own experience.

ACTIVITY

Give each child a **Friends Are to Help reproducible (page 55)**. Have children think about and discuss times when they needed help and their friends came to the rescue. Write any key vocabulary that comes up in the discussion on **chart paper** for children to use in their writing as they complete the reproducible. Have children add illustrations, and then invite them to share their work with the class.

Little Red Hen

Directions: Think about the story. What did Little Red Hen do after planting the seeds to end up with a loaf of bread? Write about each step on a feather.

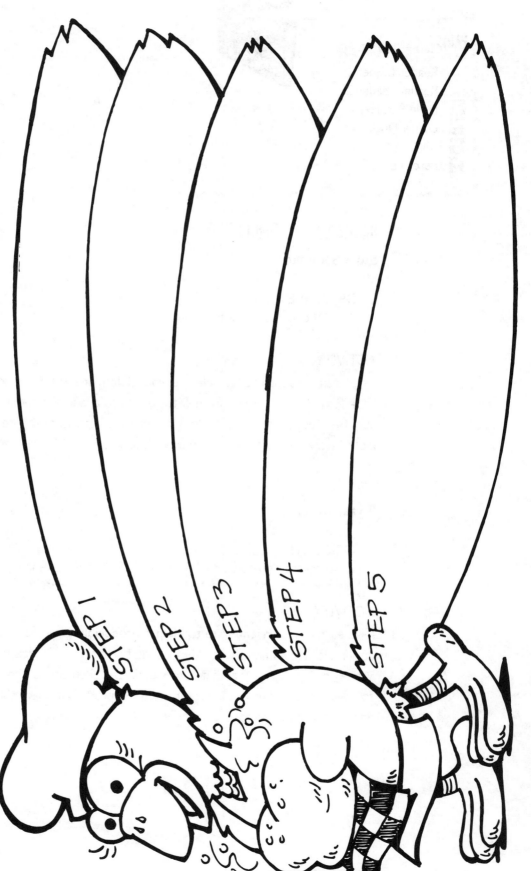

STEP 1

STEP 2

STEP 3

STEP 4

STEP 5

Fairy Tales Reader's Theater © 2004 Creative Teaching Press

Name_____ Date _____

Friends Are to Help

Directions: Write about a time you needed help. How did your friends help you? Draw a picture to illustrate your story.

ALL BY MYSELF!

Retold and adapted by Margaret Allen

Reader Leader 1: Little Red Hen lived on a farm. She shared her barnyard with her friends, Dandy Duck, Kit Cat, and Percy Pig.

Reader Leader 2: One day, while Little Red Hen was scratching for worms, she found some seeds.

Little Red Hen: Cluck, cluck. Cluckety-cluck. Look what I found! Such wonderful luck!

Reader Leader 1: Her friends Dandy Duck, Kit Cat, and Percy Pig ran over to see what Little Red Hen had found.

Little Red Hen: See? Wheat seeds. I will plant them. Who will help me plant the wheat?

Dandy Duck: Not I! Quack, quack! I'd rather draw.

Kit Cat: Not I! Meow, meow! I hurt my paw.

Percy Pig: Not I! Oink, Oink! I'll nap in my straw!

Little Red Hen: Okay! Then I will plant the wheat myself—all by myself!

Fairy Tales Reader's Theater © 2004 Creative Teaching Press

Reader Leader 2: And she did.

Little Red Hen: Cluck, cluck. Cluckety-cluck. Look what I see! Such wonderful luck!

Reader Leader 1: Her friends Dandy Duck, Kit Cat, and Percy Pig ran over to see what Little Red Hen saw.

Little Red Hen: See? It is the wheat. It has grown. Who will help me cut the wheat?

Dandy Duck: Not I! Quack, quack! I hurt my wing

Kit Cat: Not I! Meow, meow! Don't have time for a thing.

Percy Pig: Not I! Oink, oink! I'd rather sing.

Little Red Hen: Okay! Then I will cut the wheat myself—all by myself!

Reader Leader 2: And she did.

Little Red Hen: Cluck, cluck. Cluckety-cluck. Look what I have! Such wonderful luck!

Reader Leader 1: Her friends Dandy Duck, Kit Cat, and Percy Pig ran over to see what Little Red Hen had.

Little Red Hen: See? It is grains of wheat. Who will help me grind the wheat into flour?

Dandy Duck: Not I! Quack, quack! I have a bad back.

Fairy Tales Reader's Theater © 2004 Creative Teaching Press

Kit Cat: Not I! Meow, meow! That skill I lack.

Percy Pig: Not I! Oink, oink! I'm with the cat.

Little Red Hen: Okay! Then I will grind the wheat myself—all by myself!

Reader Leader 2: And she did.

Little Red Hen: Cluck, cluck. Cluckety-cluck. Look what I have! Such wonderful luck!

Reader Leader 1: Her friends Dandy Duck, Kit Cat, and Percy Pig ran over to see what Little Red Hen had.

Little Red Hen: See? It's flour. Who will help me make the bread?

Dandy Duck: Not I! Quack, quack! Where's that book I read?

Kit Cat: Not I! Meow, meow! That hurts my head!

Percy Pig: Not I! Oink, oink! I'm going back to bed.

Little Red Hen: Okay! Then I will make the bread myself—all by myself!

Reader Leader 2: And she did.

Little Red Hen: Cluck, cluck. Cluckety-cluck. Look what I have! Such wonderful luck!

Fairy Tales Reader's Theater © 2004 Creative Teaching Press

Reader Leader 1: Her friends Dandy Duck, Kit Cat, and Percy Pig ran over to see what Little Red Hen had.

Little Red Hen: See? It's fresh, hot bread. Who will help me eat the bread?

Dandy Duck: I will! Quack, quack! I love to eat.

Kit Cat: I will! Meow, meow! Hot bread is a treat.

Percy Pig: I will! Oink, oink! And I'll even be neat.

Little Red Hen: No, you will not! You did not plant the wheat. You did not cut the wheat. You did not grind the wheat. You did not make the bread. I did! By myself! All by myself! And that's how I will eat it—*all by myself!*

Reader Leader 2: And she did.

Fairy Tales Reader's Theater © 2004 Creative Teaching Press

THE TROLL BRIDGE

FAIRY TALES

Script Summary

The Troll Bridge is based on the traditional tale The Three Billy Goats Gruff. To set the stage for reading, display one chocolate chip, one snack-size chocolate bar, and one large chocolate bar. Ask children if they had a choice, which one they would choose: small, medium, or large? This is the dilemma for a character in today's story. Before reading, ask children about a troll and what they know about one. Then, ask them to listen to the story to determine if the troll made a wise decision. After reading the script to the class, connect the saying "the grass is always greener on the other side" to this tale.

Reading Rehearsal

When you read aloud the script for children, have them listen for the following:

- Write *trip trap, trip trap* on the board three times. Write it in small, thin letters, larger with thicker letters, and then very large and thick. Have children read all three using a stronger voice each time. Have them practice expressive tonal variation by rereading all three phrases from the board.

- Read the troll's voice in a bold, strong voice or a shrill, harsh voice, and have children discuss which they prefer and why.

- Vary the voices of the three billy goats to suggest size and age with your voice. Have children discuss the differences and mimic your reading.

PARTS

Reader Leader 1
Reader Leader 2
Troll
Max Gruff
Ben Gruff
Milo Gruff

DRAMA COACH'S CORNER

Finding the Setting

OBJECTIVE
Visualize and write about the story scene.

ACTIVITY

Give each child a **Troll Bridge reproducible (page 62)**. Lead children in a guided visualization of Troll and Troll Bridge. Ask them to think about how Troll looks, feels, and moves about under Troll Bridge. Have them open their eyes and use their conception of Troll to complete the reproducible. Invite children to share their completed work with the class.

Retell the Story

OBJECTIVE
Use stick puppets to retell the story.

ACTIVITY

Give each child a **Gruff and Troll reproducible (page 63)**. Have children color and cut out the figures, glue them onto **craft sticks,** and use their stick puppets to retell the story. Have children make a "setting bag" by cutting the top of a **paper lunch sack** to resemble a bridge. Invite them to keep their character stick puppets in the bag.

Name_____ Date _____

Troll Bridge

Directions: Think about how a troll might look. Draw your idea of Troll living under Troll Bridge.

Fairy Tales Reader's Theater © 2004 Creative Teaching Press

Gruff and Troll

Directions: Color and cut out the characters. Glue them onto craft sticks. Use your stick puppets to retell the story of *The Troll Bridge.*

Fairy Tales Reader's Theater © 2004 Creative Teaching Press

THE TROLL BRIDGE

Retold and adapted by Margaret Allen

PARTS

Reader Leader 1
Reader Leader 2
Troll
Max Gruff
Ben Gruff
Milo Gruff

Reader Leader 1: The Billy Goats Gruff brothers lived on one side of a hill. Max was the oldest and the biggest. Milo was the youngest and the smallest. And Ben was in-between.

Reader Leader 2: Every day they ate grass on their side of the hill. Every day they looked across to the other side. The grass on that side looked much greener!

Max: That grass looks so much better than ours. I want to eat *that* grass!

Ben: Calm down, Max. You know we can't.

Max: And why not, I ask you?

Milo: Because first we would have to cross the Troll Bridge. That's why!

Max: Then today is the day! I'm going. Are you two coming with me?

Ben: That grass *does* look very tasty!

Milo: Okay. Count me in.

Fairy Tales Reader's Theater © 2004 Creative Teaching Press

THE TROLL BRIDGE

Max: But just in case of trouble, I better stay here. Then, if you need me, just call. I will come running. Milo, you go first. Then Ben will go.

Milo: Why me first?

Max: Troll won't mess with you. You're too little!

Ben and Max: Ha, ha, ha!

Reader Leader 1: So Milo Gruff started to cross the Troll Bridge. Trip, trap. Trip, trap.

Reader Leader 2: The Troll spoke in his great big voice.

Troll: Who is that on my Troll Bridge?

Milo: It's me, Milo Gruff.

Troll: Then I'm coming to get you!

Milo: Oh, no! Please don't do that. Wait until my brother Ben gets here. He's much bigger than I am, and tasty, too!

Troll: Bigger? Good. Then be off with you!

Reader Leader 1: And Troll went back under the Troll Bridge.

Reader Leader 2: Milo Gruff made it to the other side of the hill. The grass *was* greener there, and it was very filling! He waved to his brothers. Then he ate some more.

Fairy Tales Reader's Theater © 2004 Creative Teaching Press

THE TROLL BRIDGE

Max: Hey, look, Ben. Little brother made it over! How about that! Your turn!

Reader Leader 1: So Ben Gruff, the middle brother, started to cross the Troll Bridge. Trip, trap. Trip, trap.

Reader Leader 2: The Troll spoke in his great big voice.

Troll: Who is that on my Troll Bridge?

Ben: It's only me, Ben Gruff.

Troll: Are you the bigger one? If so, I'm coming to get you!

Ben: That depends on what you mean by bigger! I mean, I am bigger than, say, a fly, but not even close to the size of my big brother, Max! Wait until he gets here! We call him Max because he is the maximum goat allowable by law!

Troll: Maximum Max? Hmmm, okay, be off with you!

Reader Leader 1: And Troll went back under the Troll Bridge.

Reader Leader 2: Ben Gruff made it to the other side of the hill. He ran to find Milo. The grass *was* greener there, and it was very filling! He waved to his brother Max. Then he ate some more.

Fairy Tales Reader's Theater © 2004 Creative Teaching Press

The Troll Bridge

Max: What about that! My brothers made it over the Troll Bridge. Guess it's *my* turn now. Look out, Troll, here I come!

Reader Leader 1: So Max Gruff, the biggest brother, started to cross the Troll Bridge. TRIP, TRAP! TRIP, TRAP!

Reader Leader 2: The Troll spoke in his great big voice.

Troll: Who is that on my Troll Bridge?

Max: It's me, Big Brother Gruff. Who are you?!?

Troll: Ahhhh! The one I waited for! You are Maximum Max, right? If so, I'm coming to get you!

Reader Leader 1: And the ugly Troll came out from under his Troll Bridge.

Troll: Here I come!

Max: Have we met? Because I have two sharp horns to poke your nose. Many sharp teeth to bite and tear. Big, pointy hooves to kick you to tomorrow!

Reader Leader 2: Troll didn't believe him. Troll swaggered to the middle of the bridge. He stood in front of Max Gruff.

THE TROLL BRIDGE

Max: Come on, Troll. Come and get me! Too long we have stayed on this side of the hill. Too long we have looked at that green grass. Too long we have feared you! Today is the day it ends!

Reader Leader 1: With that, Max Gruff butted Troll with his horns. Then he kicked Troll into tomorrow!

Reader Leader 2: And that was the end of Troll and Troll Bridge. The big ugly Troll came down on the other side of the mountain. He was never seen or heard of again.

Reader Leader 1: And the Billy Goats Gruff? Max, Ben, and Milo went up to the hillside to eat as much green grass as they wanted. And, for all I know, they are still there!

Fairy Tales Reader's Theater © 2004 Creative Teaching Press

TWICE AS
NICE!

FAIRY TALES

SCRIPT SUMMARY

Twice as Nice! is based on the fable The Town Mouse and the Country Mouse. The moral is, "Poverty with security is better than plenty in the midst of fear and uncertainty." Ask children if they have been to the country. What did they experience there? Ask if they have been to the city. What did they experience there? Was there a difference in the two places? This script highlights the differences in two cousins' lives—one in the country, the other in the city.

READING REHEARSAL

When you read aloud the script for children, have them listen for the following:

• Model Connie Country Mouse's "countrified" voice, perhaps overexaggerating it a bit. Have children repeat each line after you in the same character voice. Have children notice that her pace is rather slow. She may even add some extra syllables to a few words to draw them out in a country drawl.

• Model Sydney City Mouse's sophisticated, even haughty, voice. Point out that her faster way of life may be reflected in a faster pace of speaking. Her diction is crisp. She does not draw out words.

PARTS

Reader Leader 1
Reader Leader 2
Reader Leader 3
Sydney City Mouse
Connie Country Mouse

Drama Coach's Corner

Compare and Contrast

OBJECTIVE
Compare and contrast the two story settings and characters.

ACTIVITY

Give each child a **City Life and Country Life reproducible (page 71)** and a **City Mouse and Country Mouse reproducible (page 72)**. Ask children to recall the introductory conversation the class had about life in the country versus life in the city. Have children write, draw, or cut out of magazines items and activities that represent city and country life and complete the City Life and Country Life reproducible. Then, invite children to use the Venn diagram on the City Mouse and Country Mouse reproducible to compare and contrast the two mice. Have them write the similarities of the two mice in the middle section and differences in the other two parts of the graphic organizer.

Name_____   Date _____

City Life and Country Life

Directions: Think about activities, places, sights, and sounds in the city. Draw, write about, or cut out pictures to represent city life on the left side of the chart. Do the same for country life on the right side.

 **City Life** | **Country Life**

Name _____

Date _____

City Mouse and Country Mouse

Directions: Think about Sydney City Mouse and Connie Country Mouse. Write about each character in the space provided. Write things they have in common in the middle part of the Venn diagram.

Sydney City Mouse

Connie Country Mouse

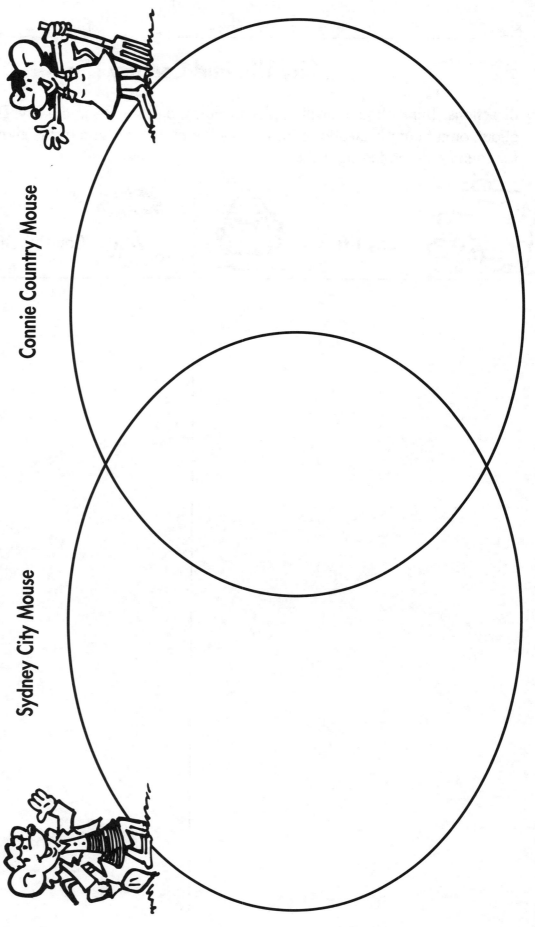

Fairy Tales Reader's Theater © 2004 Creative Teaching Press

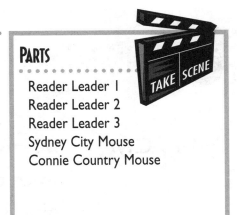

TWICE AS NICE!

Retold and adapted by Margaret Allen

PARTS

Reader Leader 1
Reader Leader 2
Reader Leader 3
Sydney City Mouse
Connie Country Mouse

Reader Leader 1: One summer day, Sydney City Mouse went to visit her cousin, Connie Country Mouse.

Reader Leader 2: Connie was very happy to see Sydney. Connie gave her a great big hug. Then, she chatted away . . .

Connie Country: Why, Sydney City Mouse, welcome to the country. We all are so glad you came for a visit, hon.

Reader Leader 3: Connie called everyone "hon"—short for "honey."

Sydney City: I'm glad to be here. But you country folks have lots of bugs! I swatted two already!

Connie Country: Just part of country livin', hon! Now, let's eat.

Reader Leader 1: Connie spread out her old red and white check tablecloth. It was her best. She set out two tiny plates. Then Connie put bread crumbs and a tiny piece of cheese on each plate.

Connie Country: Dig in, hon! Mighty tasty!

TWICE AS NICE!

Sydney City: Mighty tasty? I think not! The food in the city is twice as nice. The tablecloths in the city are twice as nice. The plates in the city are twice as nice. City life is twice as nice as country life! And, we don't have all these bugs!

Connie Country: Twice as nice? Maybe I should go to the city with you. But, it's bedtime now. Let's sleep on it.

Reader Leader 2: Connie didn't say "hon" this time! Connie's feelings were hurt. But Connie did not stay hurt or mad for long. She was very forgiving.

Reader Leader 3: Connie and Sydney nestled into old matchboxes filled with lumps of straw.

Connie Country: I guess your beds are twice as nice in the city.

Sydney City: Our beds? At least twice as nice! Oh, well. Let's try to sleep. That is, if I can *ever* flatten these lumps!

Reader Leader 1: The mouse cousins were soon asleep.

Reader Leader 2: Connie had a dream. She dreamed she went with Sydney to the city. She dreamed about a fancy house. She dreamed about a fancy bed. And, she dreamed about all that fancy food.

Reader Leader 3: At sunrise, Connie woke up. She went over to Sydney's bed. She shook her cousin.

Fairy Tales Reader's Theater © 2004 Creative Teaching Press

TWICE AS NICE!

Connie Country: Sydney, we slept late! Let's get up.

Sydney City: Late? The sun is barely up! Oh well, at least I can get out of this lumpy bed.

Connie Country: Sydney, last night I dreamed about the city. I will go back with you!

Sydney City: Good! Let's get dressed and leave soon! And please, wear your *best* clothes. You are going to the city now!

Reader Leader 1: Connie put on her *best* dress. Sydney's dress was twice as nice, of course.

Reader Leader 2: By sundown, the cousins had reached the city.

Sydney City: Well, cousin. Here is my home! What do you think?

Connie Country: Oh, Sydney. It *is* twice as nice!

Sydney City: Let's eat. I am hungry!

Reader Leader 3: Sydney put out her fancy tablecloth. She put out her fancy plates. She filled them with fancy food. The cousins sat down to eat.

Connie Country: Oh, Sydney. This tablecloth is twice as nice, hon! And this plate! And this food, oh, this food . . . Why, I could eat and eat and . . .

Reader Leader 1: All of a sudden, Connie stopped her chatting. She heard a meow, a loud meow.

Fairy Tales Reader's Theater © 2004 Creative Teaching Press

Sydney City: Oh, no! It's the cat. Someone let the cat in. Run for your life!

Reader Leader 2: Poor Connie did not know what to do. She followed Sydney down a mouse hole.

Connie Country: Does this happen very often?

Sydney City: Oh, it's nothing, really, Connie dear. You will get used to it. Look, it's all safe now. Let's go eat.

Reader Leader 3: Connie and Sydney went back to the table. They ate a few bites. Then, all of a sudden, they heard a bark, a LOUD bark.

Sydney City: Oh, no! It's the dog. Someone let the dog in. Run for your life!

Reader Leader 1: Poor Connie. She was so upset. But this time she knew what to do. She followed Sydney down the same mouse hole.

Connie Country: Is this how your city life is?

Sydney City: Oh, it's nothing, really, Connie dear. You will get used to it. Look. All safe now. Let's go eat.

Connie Country: I don't think so, Sydney! You made me believe your life is nicer than my life.

Sydney City: Well, *it is!* At least twice as nice!

Connie Country: Yes, your *house* is twice as nice. Your *tablecloth* is twice as nice. Your *plate* is twice as nice as mine. And your food is even *three* times nicer than mine. But I don't like your life! I like *my life.* I am going home! Home to my simple *safe* life! Good-bye, hon!

Reader Leader 2: With that, Connie took her things and headed home.

Reader Leader 3: When she got there, it was very late. She crawled into her little matchbox filled with hay. She quickly went to sleep.

Reader Leader 1: At sunup, Connie got up. She put out her red and white check tablecloth. She put out her plate. She put bread crumbs and a small piece of cheese on the plate. Then she ate.

Connie Country: I think it is *my* life that is twice as nice! It may be simple, but it is safe!

Reader Leader 2: And Connie Country never went back to the city again.

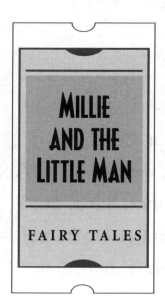

MILLIE AND THE LITTLE MAN

FAIRY TALES

SCRIPT SUMMARY

Millie and the Little Man is based on the fairy tale Rumpelstiltskin. Display straw (taken from a broom or real straw) and coins. Ask if there is a way to turn the straw into money. Tell children that this script is about a character who could turn straw into gold. Write the word *Rumpelstiltskin* on the board, and pronounce it.

READING REHEARSAL

When you read aloud the script for children, have them listen for the following:

- Millie's voice is low and she speaks slowly when she is sad that she cannot spin straw into gold. She should sound disappointed. Her sentences will fall at the end.

- Point out that the Little Man may have a "little" voice as well. Write on the board the Little Man's part when he reveals his name. Have children practice the rhyme with great expression.

PARTS

- Reader Leader 1
- Reader Leader 2
- Reader Leader 3
- The Little Man
- Millie Miller
- Mr. Miller
- King Rex

DRAMA COACH'S CORNER

Class Flip Book

> **OBJECTIVE**
> Illustrate and describe a character from the story.

ACTIVITY

Give each child a **Character Flip Book reproducible (page 80).** Ask children to select a character from the story and draw each part of it as directed on the page. Have them write to the left of their drawing. Combine the pages into a class flip book.

Identify the Details

> **OBJECTIVE**
> Identify the story elements.

ACTIVITY

Give each child a **Golden Story Details reproducible (page 81).** Have children discuss each of the story elements listed on the page. After you have discussed each element, provide time for children to record the information on the page. Write difficult words on the board, as needed.

Character Flip Book

Directions: Select a character from the story. Write your responses in each section. Then draw the character's head in Section A. Start drawing the neck at the two small dots. Draw the midsection of the body in Section B. Start at the small dots and end at the large dots. Draw the rest of the body in Section C.

Ⓐ Who?

Describe and name the character.

Ⓑ What?

Describe something the character did.

Ⓒ Where?

Describe where the character is.

Golden Story Details

Directions: Think about the story. Write details about the story on each gold coin. Find a partner and discuss the story.

Main character

Problem

Other Characters

Best Part of Story

Solution:

Title:_____

MILLIE AND THE LITTLE MAN
Retold and adapted by Margaret Allen

PARTS
Reader Leader 1
Reader Leader 2
Reader Leader 3
The Little Man
Millie Miller
Mr. Miller
King Rex

Reader Leader 1: In the days of kings and queens, there was a poor man named Mr. Miller. He worked all day at a mill, grinding wheat into flour.

Reader Leader 2: Mr. Miller's work was hard. It was the same thing day after day. Only his daughter Millie brought him joy.

Reader Leader 3: Millie was a beautiful girl. Mr. Miller was very proud of her. Sometimes he would brag about her. Some of the things he said were not even true. One day he bragged that Millie could spin straw into gold.

King Rex: What did you say, Mr. Miller? Your daughter can spin straw into gold? I *love* gold. If it is so, I would like to meet her.

Mr. Miller: Oh yes, King Rex. It is so. When would you like to meet her?

King Rex: Bring her to my castle tonight. I will give her a test.

Fairy Tales Reader's Theater © 2004 Creative Teaching Press

MILLIE AND THE LITTLE MAN

Reader Leader 1: Mr. Miller ran home from work. He told Millie what happened.

Mr. Miller: So you must go. You must pass his test.

Millie: But, Father, I cannot spin straw into gold! What will I do?

Reader Leader 2: Mr. Miller took Millie to King Rex. King Rex put her in a small room filled with straw.

King Rex: Now spin, my dear Millie. Spin this straw into gold. But if you cannot, I will put your father in jail for the rest of his life for his lies!

Reader Leader 3: King Rex left Millie alone. She began to cry and cry. What could she do? All of a sudden, the door opened. A strange little man walked into the room.

The Little Man: Good evening, Millie. Why are you crying?

Millie: King Rex said I must spin this straw into gold. If I do not, he will put my father in jail forever.

The Little Man: What will you give me if I spin this straw into gold?

Millie: What? Will you? I will give you my gold necklace.

The Little Man: Step back. I will do it for you.

Fairy Tales Reader's Theater © 2004 Creative Teaching Press

MILLIE AND THE LITTLE MAN

Reader Leader 1: The Little Man worked all night. By morning, all of the straw had been spun into gold. Then, the Little Man left as suddenly as he came. King Rex opened the door. His mouth fell open! He saw gold! Lots of gold!

King Rex: Well, Millie, it is true! You are amazing. I love gold! But come with me. Your test is not over yet.

Reader Leader 2: King Rex took Millie to a bigger room with more straw. He told her to get to work. Again, Millie cried and cried. Again the door opened and the Little Man walked in.

The Little Man: And why are you crying now? Didn't I spin the straw into gold for you?

Millie: Yes, you did. But King Rex wants more!

The Little Man: I can spin this straw into gold for you. But what will you give me this time?

Millie: I will give you my gold ring.

The Little Man: Step back. I will do it for you.

Fairy Tales Reader's Theater © 2004 Creative Teaching Press

MILLIE AND THE LITTLE MAN

Reader Leader 3: Again the Little Man worked all night. By morning. all of the straw had been spun into gold. King Rex was overjoyed! He took Millie and put her into the largest room in his castle.

King Rex: One more test, Millie dear. Spin this into gold, and your father will be safe!

Reader Leader 1: Millie began to cry harder than ever. The door opened. In walked the Little Man.

The Little Man: He wants *more* gold? Tell me, what will you give me this time if I do it for you?

Millie: I have nothing left.

The Little Man: Promise me that if you become queen, you will give me your first child.

Millie: I do not think I will ever be queen, Little Man. So, yes, I guess that is a safe promise.

Reader Leader 2: The Little Man kept his word. He spun all of the straw into gold by morning. When King Rex saw all of the gold, he was very happy. To Millie's surprise, he made her his queen the very next day. She became Queen Millie.

MILLIE AND THE LITTLE MAN

Reader Leader 3: Believe it or not, Millie was very happy. A year later she had her first baby. She did not think any more about the Little Man. Not until one day, when the door popped open. In walked the Little Man.

The Little Man: Hello, Queen Millie. I am here for the child.

Millie: What? Surely you will not take my baby. I will pay you lots of money. I am Queen Millie now. King Rex will give money to me. Please do not take my baby!

The Little Man: I am sorry, Queen Millie. A promise is a promise. I want the child.

Reader Leader 1: Millie cried and cried and begged and begged. The Little Man felt sorry for her.

The Little Man: Okay. I will give you three days. If you can guess my name in three days, the baby stays with you. If not, I get the baby.

Reader Leader 2: For the next two days, Millie guessed every name she had ever heard. Each time she guessed, the Little Man told her that was not his name. She didn't know what to do, so she sent a servant into the woods to find new names.

Fairy Tales Reader's Theater © 2004 Creative Teaching Press

MILLIE AND THE LITTLE MAN

Reader Leader 3: As luck would have it, the servant came upon a campfire in the woods. He saw a little man dancing. He heard what the man said.

The Little Man: Ha, ha, ha! Hee, hee, hee. I will soon have the queen's baby. What a pity! What a shame! She doesn't know—Rumpelstiltskin is my name!

Reader Leader 1: The servant ran back to the castle. He told Queen Millie what he saw and what he heard. The next day Queen Millie saw the Little Man.

Queen Millie: Let's see. Is your name Harry? Simon? Krispen? No? Then is your name . . . Rumpelstiltskin?

Reader Leader 2: The Little Man screamed. He jumped up and down. Then he ran as far away as he could. And that was the last Queen Millie ever saw of Rumpelstiltskin!

**TO KISS
A FROG**

FAIRY TALES

SCRIPT SUMMARY

To Kiss a Frog is based on the fairy tale The Frog Prince. Ask children if they have ever seen a television show in which one person plays two characters. In this script, one character turns into another character! Also, ask children if they believe that a promise is a promise. A character in this story isn't sure—because it means having to kiss a frog!!

READING REHEARSAL

When you read aloud the script for children, have them listen for the following:

- The King's age and authority are communicated in a deep voice. Have children imitate your reading word for word.

- Invite children to consider how a frog would sound. His pace may speed up when he is trying to convince the princess to do something she does not want to do.

- The princess is very young in the story. The tone of her voice is quite high to reflect her age and gender.

PARTS

Reader Leader 1
Reader Leader 2
Reader Leader 3
⬆ Princess Pansy
⬆ The Frog
The King

DRAMA COACH'S CORNER

Sequencing the Story

OBJECTIVE
Sequence the main events of the story.

ACTIVITY

Give each child a set of **Story Sequencing Cards (page 90).** Have children color and cut out the six picture cards, sequence them correctly, and retell the story. When you have checked their work, have them glue the cards to **construction paper** in the correct order.

The Frog

OBJECTIVE
Discuss and visualize the character of the frog prince.

ACTIVITY

Give each child a **Before and After reproducible (page 91).** Have children discuss the frog and his change into a frog prince. Then, ask them to draw their version of each character.

Story Sequencing Cards

Directions: Color the cards, cut them apart, and place them in order to retell the story *To Kiss a Frog.*

Before and After

Directions: Complete the pictures to make the frog and the prince.

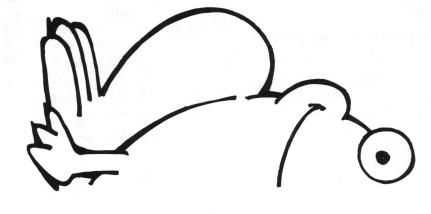

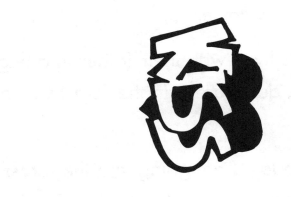

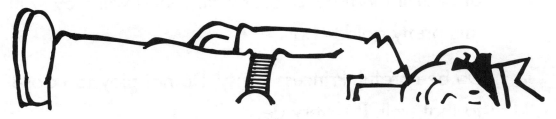

TO KISS A FROG

Retold and adapted by Margaret Allen

PARTS

Reader Leader 1
Reader Leader 2
Reader Leader 3
Princess Pansy
The Frog
The King

Reader Leader 1: In a kingdom long ago, there was a kind king with three lovely daughters: Rose, Iris, and Pansy.

Reader Leader 2: The youngest daughter was the prettiest. Her name was Princess Pansy because she was as pretty as her father's favorite flower.

Reader Leader 3: All three girls lived with their father in a huge castle near a deep, dark forest. In the forest was a deep, cool well.

Princess Pansy: It is so hot today. I am going into the forest. I will drink from that deep, cool well. Then I will play with this pretty golden ball.

The King: Do be careful, Princess Pansy. Do not play too close to that well. It is very deep.

Princess Pansy: Okay, Father.

Reader Leader 1: But Princess Pansy did play too close to the well. She tossed her golden ball up and caught it. Up and caught it. Up and . . .

Fairy Tales Reader's Theater © 2004 Creative Teaching Press

 **TO KISS A FROG**

Princess Pansy: Oh, no! My golden ball has fallen into the well. It will be lost forever!

Reader Leader 2: Princess Pansy started to cry. She had lost her ball and her father would be upset. She cried and cried.

The Frog: Why are you crying, lovely princess?

Reader Leader 3: The princess looked up.

Princess Pansy: Who is there? Who is talking to me?

The Frog: It is I. Why are you crying?

Princess Pansy: I lost my golden ball in the well.

The Frog: Don't cry, lovely princess. I will fetch your ball. But what will you give me when I get it back for you?

Princess Pansy: Whatever you wish, dear frog: my ring, my necklace, even my crown.

The Frog: What can I do with those? I will get your golden ball for you if you will do three things for me.

Princess Pansy: What three things, dear frog?

The Frog: Be my friend. Let me eat and drink from your golden plate and cup at dinner. And give me a little good-night kiss. If you will do these three things, I will get your ball for you.

Fairy Tales Reader's Theater © 2004 Creative Teaching Press

Princess Pansy: Yes, oh, sure, whatever you like.

Reader Leader 1:   Princess Pansy agreed. But she did not think the frog really meant what he was asking. Why would a frog want to live with people? Why eat from her plate, drink from her cup, and kiss her? That made no sense.

Reader Leader 2:   The frog dove into the deep well. Soon he popped up with the golden ball in his mouth. He hopped out of the well and gave the princess her ball.

Reader Leader 3:   Without even saying "thank you," the princess ran back to the castle.

The Frog: Wait! Wait, Princess Pansy! I cannot keep up with you. You promised to be my friend. You promised to take me home with you. You are running too fast. I can't keep up!

Reader Leader 1:   Princess Pansy did not even turn around. She ran home and forgot all about the frog.

Reader Leader 2:   The next day, the king and his three daughters were eating dinner. They heard a strange sound: plip, plop, plip, plop, plip, plop.

The King: What is that sound?

Fairy Tales Reader's Theater © 2004 Creative Teaching Press

TO KISS A FROG

The Frog: It is I, King, Princess Pansy's new friend.

The King: Princess Pansy, your new frog . . . um . . . friend is here.

Princess Pansy: Oh, Father, I am so sorry. I played too close to the well. My golden ball went in. That frog got it out for me. He asked me to make some silly promises to get it back.

The King: Silly promises? What about a silly golden ball? Whatever you promised, you must honor. We keep our word, no matter what! Now, what did you promise?

The Frog: Oh, great King, thank you! She promised to be my friend. She promised to let me eat from her golden plate and drink from her golden cup. And she promised to give me a little good-night kiss!

Princess Pansy: Oh, Father. You aren't going to make me do those things, are you?

The King: Princess Pansy, when a person helps you when you are in need, you must repay him or her.

Reader Leader 3: So that night the frog ate from her plate, drank from her cup, and got his good-night kiss. In the morning, he hopped away.

Fairy Tales Reader's Theater © 2004 Creative Teaching Press

Princess Pansy: That wasn't so bad. At least he's a neat and polite frog.

Reader Leader 1: Each night for two more nights, the frog returned. He ate from her plate, drank from her cup, and got a good-night kiss. Each evening they played a game of checkers.

Reader Leader 2: On the third morning, when Princess Pansy woke up, she did not see an ugly frog looking at her. Instead, there was a handsome young prince smiling at her.

Princess Pansy: Who are you? And what are you doing here?

The Frog: Dear princess, it is me, the frog! I am really a prince who was under a spell. You have broken that spell! You were my friend for three days. You let me eat and drink with you, and you gave me a good-night kiss. *That* is what freed me from the spell! Your third kiss! Will you marry me, dear Princess Pansy?

Reader Leader 3: Princess Pansy said yes. The King gave them his blessings. And when Princess Pansy and her frog . . . I mean, her prince, were old enough, they were married.

Reader Leader 1: The two lived a very long and happy life together!

Fairy Tales Reader's Theater © 2004 Creative Teaching Press